Soccer Gift Books for Kids Ages 6-12:
500 Soccer Fact Quizzes for Kids

Table of Contents

- Table of Contents 2
- Introduction 3
- How to Use the Book 5
- How The Trackers Work 6
- Basic Soccer Rules 10
- Soccer Legends 13
- Current Soccer Players 15
- Soccer Clubs 15
- World Cup Soccer 21
- Soccer in USA 23
- History of Soccer 25
- Soccer Mascots 28
- Soccer World Records 31
- Soccer Stadiums 35
- Soccer Technology 38
- Soccer Positions 41
- Messi and Ronaldo 43
- Soccer Moves 45
- Soccer Gear 47
- Soccer Fitness/Injury 48
- Answers 50
- APPENDIX 73

Disclaimer

Copyright © 2025

All Rights Reserved

No part of this eBook can be transmitted or reproduced in any form including print, electronic, photocopying, scanning, mechanical, or recording without prior written permission from the author.

Introduction

Soccer is one of the fastest-growing sports in the U.S. and the most popular sport globally. Even in countries like Australia, the U.S., and China, where it's not the dominant sport, it's gaining significant traction, especially among younger generations.

If you're reading this, you're either among the millions of soccer fans in the U.S. or one of the billions worldwide. Maybe you're just trying to learn more about soccer while having some fun along the way.

This book is designed to be interactive, offering readers a chance to learn about soccer's history, legends, and trivia. It's also structured as a quiz game, perfect for groups of soccer fans. There's a scorecard provided for up to 8 players (use pencil for reusability). Whether you're a soccer novice or a seasoned fan, this book offers something for everyone.

How to Use the Book

The book contains 500 numbered quiz questions, ideal for one-on-one or group quizzes. You can even form teams, making it a perfect addition to a Premier League viewing party.

We recommend using the provided soccer trackers, which allow for repeat usage if filled in with pencil. You can also print additional quiz templates from the book for continued play.

How The Trackers Work

On the next page, you'll find 3 score trackers. Each tracker accommodates up to 8 players/teams, and each participant answers 10 rounds of questions. The topic for each question is listed on the second row of the tracker.

- Each player/team gets 30 seconds to answer their question. A correct answer earns 10 points.

- If they fail to answer, the question opens up to all teams for an additional 15 seconds. A correct response from another team earns 5 points.

Need more trackers? Check the Appendix for extra templates.

Participant/Team Name / Team Name	Round 1 Basic Soccer	Round 2 Legends	Round 3 Clubs	Round 4 World Cup	Round 5 US Soccer	Round 6 World Rec	Round 7 Stadiums	Round 8 Technology	Round 9 Messi/Ronaldo	Round 10 Positions	Total
1											
2											
3											
4											
5											
6											
7											
8											

Participant/Team Name / Team Name	Round 1 Basic Soccer	Round 2 Legends	Round 3 Clubs	Round 4 World Cup	Round 5 US Soccer	Round 6 World Rec	Round 7 Stadiums	Round 8 Technology	Round 9 Messi/Ronaldo	Round 10 Positions	Total
1											
2											
3											
4											
5											
6											
7											
8											

Participant/Team Name / Team Name	Round 1 Basic Soccer	Round 2 Legends	Round 3 Clubs	Round 4 World Cup	Round 5 US Soccer	Round 6 World Rec	Round 7 Stadiums	Round 8 Technology	Round 9 Messi/Ronaldo	Round 10 Positions	Total
1											
2											
3											
4											
5											
6											
7											
8											

Below is an example of a tracker filled out for 3 people competing against each other. They get 10 points for each correct answer directed to them. If they get it wrong, they get 0 points, and the questions go out to the other groups. If any of the other groups get the answer, they get an additional 5 points.

Participant/Team	Name / Team	Round 1	Round 2	Round 3	Round 4	Round 5	Round 6	Round 7	Round 8	Round 9	Round 10	Total
		Basic Soccer	Legends	Clubs	World Cup	US Soccer	World Rec	Stadiums	Technology	Messi/Ronaldo	Positions	
1	Steve	10	0	0	0	0	0	10+5+5	0	10	10	50
2	Bob	0	0	10+5+5	10	0	0	0	10	10	0	40
3	Sam	0	0	0	0	0	10	0	0	10	0	20
4												
5												
6												
7												
8												

Basic Soccer Rules

1. How long does a standard soccer match last?
2. How many players can each team have on the field at a time?
3. When does a goal count?
4. When is a throw-in awarded?
5. Who can handle the ball within their own penalty area?
6. When is a penalty kick awarded?
7. How far is the penalty spot from the center of the goal?
8. What is an own goal?
9. What must happen for an indirect free kick to count as a goal?
10. What do yellow and red cards signify?
11. What happens if a player receives two yellow cards in a game?
12. When is a goal kick awarded?
13. What is the radius of the center circle?
14. What constitutes a handball?
15. What are the dimensions of a standard soccer field?
16. Can players be offside in their own half of the field?
17. How many players are allowed on a team's roster for a match?
18. What is the minimum number of players a team must have to start a match?
19. How long is extra time in knockout matches?
20. What happens if the score is still tied after extra time?

21. How long does a goalkeeper have to release the ball?
22. What is the "advantage rule"?
23. How far must opposing players be from the ball during a free kick?
24. What is a "drop ball"?
25. Can a goal be scored directly from a kick-off?
26. How many referees are typically on the field during a professional match?
27. What is the fourth official's primary role?
28. Can a player be offside from a throw-in?
29. What is the maximum thickness of the goal posts and crossbar?
30. How is playing time extended beyond the 90 minutes?
31. What is a "professional foul"?
32. Can a player score an own goal from a free kick?
33. What is the "second touch" rule on free kicks?
34. Can a goalkeeper be penalized for handling a back-pass?
35. What is a "quick free kick"?
36. Can a player be offside from a goal kick?
37. What is the "wall" in soccer?
38. How many touches are allowed on a kick-off?
39. Can a referee change a decision after play has restarted?
40. Can a substitute take a penalty in a shootout without having played in the match?

41. What is the maximum number of substitutions allowed in most professional matches?
42. Can a player be sent off before the match starts?
43. What does VAR stand for?
44. When can VAR be used?

Soccer Legends

45. Which Brazilian player is often referred to as "The King of Football"?
46. Who is the all-time top scorer in World Cup history?
47. Which Dutch player was known as "The Flying Dutchman"?
48. Who won the Ballon d'Or a record seven times?
49. Which goalkeeper is nicknamed "The Black Spider"?
50. Who is known as "The Divine Ponytail"?
51. Which English striker is nicknamed "The Hurricane"?
52. Who is considered "The White Pelé"?
53. Which Argentine player is known as "El Pibe de Oro" (The Golden Boy)?
54. Who is the only player to have won the World Cup three times?
55. Which Portuguese Manager is nicknamed "The Special One"?
56. Who is known as "Der Bomber"?
57. Which Italian defender is nicknamed "The Berlin Wall"?
58. Who is the player who has scored the most goals in football history?
59. Which French player is known as "Le Roi"?
60. Who is nicknamed "The Galloping Major"?
61. Which Brazilian striker is known as "O Fenômeno"?
62. Who is the only player to have won three World Cup finals?

63. Which Dutch player is known as "The Total Footballer"?

64. Who is nicknamed "The Egyptian King"?

65. Which English player is known as "Gazza"?

66. Who is the oldest player to score in a World Cup?

67. The least populated country to have won a world cup.

68. Who is nicknamed "The Kaiser"?

69. Which Portuguese player is known as "The Black Panther"?

70. Who is the all-time top scorer for the Brazilian national team?

71. Which Italian goalkeeper is nicknamed "Gigi"?

72. Who is known as "The Atomic Flea"?

73. Which French player is nicknamed "Zizou"?

74. Who is the youngest player to score in a World Cup final?

Current Soccer Players

75. Which Portuguese forward currently plays for Al Nassr and is considered one of the greatest players of all time?
76. Who is the Argentine forward for Inter Miami CF, known for his incredible dribbling skills and numerous Ballon d'Or wins?
77. Which Norwegian striker, known for his goal-scoring prowess, currently plays for Manchester City?
78. Who is the French forward for Paris Saint-Germain, famous for his speed and technique?
79. Which Egyptian forward is Liverpool's top scorer and has won multiple Premier League Golden Boots?
80. Who is the Belgian midfielder for Manchester City, known for his playmaking abilities?
81. Which Polish striker currently plays for Barcelona after a successful career at Bayern Munich?
82. Who is the Brazilian forward for Real Madrid, known for his flair and dribbling skills?
83. Which English striker, captain of the England national team, had a long career at Tottenham Hotspur before moving to Bayern Munich in 2023?
84. Who is the German goalkeeper for Bayern Munich, considered one of the best in his position?

85. Which French midfielder plays for Juventus and won the World Cup with France in 2018?
86. Who is the Dutch defender for Liverpool, known for his leadership and aerial ability?
87. Which Belgian forward, after a long stint at Chelsea, played for Real Madrid until 2023 and then retired from football at age 32?
88. Who is the Italian goalkeeper for Paris Saint-Germain, famous for his long career with Juventus and the Italian national team?
89. Which Portuguese midfielder plays for Manchester United and is known for his creativity?
90. Who is the Spanish midfielder for Manchester City, known for his passing ability and vision?
91. Which Senegalese forward left Liverpool for Bayern Munich in 2022, before moving on to Al Nassr in 2023?
92. Who is the French defender for Real Madrid, known for his pace and defensive skills?
93. Which Argentine forward, known for his dribbling and free-kicks, spent the 2022–23 season at Juventus and then returned to play for Benfica in 2023?
94. Which English right-back, famed for his attacking play, starred for Liverpool and moved to Real Madrid in 2025?
95. Which Brazilian goalkeeper plays for Liverpool and is known for his distribution skills?

96. Who is the Croatian midfielder for Real Madrid, known for his passing range and vision?
97. Which French defender plays for Manchester United and won the World Cup with France in 2018?
98. Who is the Portuguese defender for Manchester City, known for his versatility and ball-playing ability?
99. Which German forward plays for Bayern Munich and is known for his versatility across the front line?
100. Who is the Spanish midfielder for Barcelona, considered one of the best young talents in world football?
101. Which English midfielder plays for Borussia Dortmund and then joined Real Madrid in 2023, is known for his creativity and dribbling skills?
102. Who is the Dutch forward for Liverpool, known for his speed and finishing ability?
103. Which Italian midfielder formerly of PSG, now at Al-Arabi in Qatar, is known for his vision and passing ability?
104. Who is the Belgian goalkeeper for Real Madrid, considered one of the best in his position?

Soccer Clubs

105. Which English club is nicknamed "The Red Devils"?
106. Which Spanish club has won the most UEFA Champions League titles?
107. Which Italian club is known as "The Old Lady"?
108. Which German club is nicknamed "Die Roten" (The Reds)?
109. Which Dutch club has produced many world-class players through its youth academy?
110. Which Portuguese club is associated with the eagle symbol?
111. Which English club plays its home games at Anfield?
112. Which Spanish club is nicknamed "Los Blancos" (The Whites)?
113. Which Italian club plays its home games at San Siro and wears red and black stripes?
114. Which French club is owned by Qatar Sports Investments?
115. Which Scottish club (now tied with Celtic) has won the most league titles in their country?
116. Which Brazilian club is associated with Pelé?
117. Which Argentine club is known as "Los Millonarios" (The Millionaires)?
118. Which English club has Stamford Bridge as its home stadium?
119. Which Spanish club's motto is "Més que un club" (More than a club)?

120. Which German club is known for its "Yellow Wall" of fans?
121. Which Italian club is nicknamed "I Nerazzurri" (The Black and Blues)?
122. Which Turkish club is known as "The Yellow Canaries"?
123. Which English club plays its home games at the Etihad Stadium?
124. Which Spanish club is based in the Basque region and only signs Basque players?
125. Which Dutch club is nicknamed "De Godenzonen" (Sons of the Gods)?
126. Which Portuguese club is known as "The Dragons"?
127. Which Italian club has a wolf as its symbol?
128. Which German club is based in Munich and wears white and blue?
129. Which English club is nicknamed "The Gunners"?
130. Which Spanish club is based in Seville and wears green and white stripes?
131. Which French club is based in Lyon and has won seven consecutive league titles?
132. Which Scottish club plays its home games at Ibrox Stadium?
133. Which Brazilian club is known as "Timão" (Big Team)?
134. Which Argentine club is nicknamed "Boca"?
135. Which English club plays its home games at Old Trafford?

136. Which Spanish club is based in the Catalonia region and wears blue and red stripes?
137. Which Italian club is nicknamed "The Old Lady's Boyfriend"?
138. Which German club is based in Dortmund and wears yellow and black?
139. Which Dutch club is based in Rotterdam and plays its home games at De Kuip?
140. Which Portuguese club is known as "The Lions"?
141. Which English club is nicknamed "The Spurs"?
142. Which Spanish club is based in Madrid and wears red and white stripes?
143. Which Italian club is nicknamed "La Viola" (The Purple Ones)?
144. Which French club is based in Marseille and has won the Champions League?
145. Which Scottish club is nicknamed "The Boys"?
146. Which Brazilian club is known as "Mengão"?
147. Which Argentine club is nicknamed "La Academia" (The Academy)?
148. Which English club plays its home games at Villa Park?
149. Which Spanish club is based in Valencia and has a bat on its crest?
150. Which English club has won the most Premier League titles?

World Cup Soccer

151. Which country has won the most FIFA World Cup titles?
152. In what year was the first FIFA World Cup held?
153. Which player has scored the most goals in World Cup history?
154. What country hosted the 2022 FIFA World Cup?
155. Who won the Golden Ball (best player) award in the 2018 World Cup?
156. Which African country was the first to reach the World Cup quarter-finals?
157. In what year did the Women's World Cup begin?
158. Which country has appeared in the most World Cup finals without winning?
159. Who is the all-time leading scorer in Women's World Cup history?
160. Which country won the first ever World Cup in 1930?
161. What is the name of the World Cup trophy?
162. Which player has played in the most World Cup tournaments?
163. What was the official match ball called for the 2022 World Cup?
164. Which country hosted the 2002 World Cup, notable for being the first in Asia?
165. Who scored the "Hand of God" goal in the 1986 World Cup?
166. Which country has played the most World Cup matches?

167. In what year did the World Cup expand to 32 teams?
168. Who won the Golden Boot (top scorer) in the 2014 World Cup?
169. Which country hosted the first Women's World Cup?
170. What is the highest scoring game in World Cup history?
171. Which player has won the most World Cups?
172. What country hosted the 2010 World Cup, the first held in Africa?
173. Who is the youngest player to score in a World Cup final?
174. In what year was the penalty shootout introduced to decide World Cup matches?
175. Which country eliminated England in the 2022 World Cup quarter-finals?
176. Who scored the winning goal for Germany in the 2014 World Cup final?
177. Which country will host the 2026 FIFA World Cup?
178. What was unique about the 2002 World Cup in terms of hosting?
179. Who won the Golden Glove (best goalkeeper) award in the 2022 World Cup?

Soccer in the USA

180. Who was the first American to win the UEFA Champions League as a player?
181. What year did the United States host its first FIFA World Cup?
182. Which American soccer player is known as "Captain America"?
183. What is the name of the top professional soccer league in the United States?
184. Which U.S. women's national team player has won the FIFA World Player of the Year award twice?
185. In what year did the U.S. women's national team win their first FIFA Women's World Cup?
186. Which American city is home to the soccer team LA Galaxy?
187. Who is the all-time leading goal scorer for the U.S. men's national team?
188. What is the name of the trophy awarded to the MLS champion?
189. Which U.S. men's national team coach led the team to the quarterfinals of the 2002 FIFA World Cup?
190. What was the first Major League Soccer (MLS) team to win the CONCACAF Champions League?
191. Who holds the record for most goals scored in a single MLS season?

192. Which U.S. women's national team player scored the winning goal in the 1999 FIFA Women's World Cup final?
193. What is the name of the stadium where the U.S. men's national team plays most of its home games?
194. Which American player became the first to score in three consecutive FIFA World Cups?
195. Who was the first American goalkeeper to play in the English Premier League?
196. Which U.S. women's national team player has the most international caps in history?
197. What year did Major League Soccer (MLS) officially start?
198. What is the nickname of the U.S. men's national soccer team?
199. Which American soccer club won the first MLS Cup in 1996?
200. Which U.S. men's national team player scored the fastest goal in World Cup history?
201. Who was the first American player to sign with a European club?
202. What is the name of the women's professional soccer league in the United States?
203. What is the record attendance for a soccer match in the United States?

History of Soccer

204. In which country was modern soccer (association football) codified in 1863?
205. Who is credited with inventing the bicycle kick?
206. Which club is considered the oldest professional football club in the world?
207. What year was FIFA founded?
208. Who was the first player to score 1000 professional goals?
209. In what year was the offside rule first introduced?
210. Which country won the first European Championship (Euro) in 1960?
211. Who was the first African player to win the Ballon d'Or?
212. What was the first soccer video game?
213. Which English club was the first to win the treble (League, FA Cup, and Champions League)?
214. Who scored the fastest hat-trick in professional football?
215. In what year was the back-pass rule introduced in soccer?
216. Which country hosted the first World Cup outside of South America or Europe?
217. Who was the first player to be transferred for over £1 million?
218. What year did the English Premier League begin?

219. Which club has won the most European Cup/Champions League titles?
220. Who invented the "Cruyff Turn"?
221. In what year was yellow and red card system introduced in soccer?
222. Which country won the first Olympic gold medal in soccer?
223. Who was the first player to score in every minute of a soccer match?
224. What year was the first televised soccer match?
225. Which club did Pelé play for most of his career?
226. Who was the first player to win the World Cup as both a player and a coach?
227. In what year was the Champions League (formerly European Cup) established?
228. Which country invented futsal?
229. Who was the first goalkeeper to score a goal in the Premier League?
230. Which team was the first national team to win the World Cup on penalties?
231. In what year was the first Women's European Championship held?
232. Who was the first player to score 100 goals in the Champions League?

233. Which club won the first Club World Cup (in its current format)?

Soccer Mascots

234. What animal is the mascot for the England national team?
235. Which fruit was the mascot for the 2016 European Championship in France?
236. What is the name of Arsenal FC's dinosaur mascot?
237. Which big cat is Leicester City's mascot?
238. What is the name of Manchester United's red devil mascot?
239. Which bird is Crystal Palace's mascot?
240. What animal represents Watford FC?
241. Which mascot represented the 2014 FIFA World Cup in Brazil?
242. What is the name of Chelsea FC's lion mascot?
243. Which animal is Tottenham Hotspur's mascot?
244. What was the name of the mascot for the 2018 FIFA World Cup in Russia?
245. Which mythical creature is Swansea City's mascot?
246. What animal represents Derby County?
247. What is the name of West Ham United's hammer-wielding mascot?
248. Which animal is Wolverhampton Wanderers' mascot?
249. What was the mascot for the 2010 FIFA World Cup in South Africa?
250. Which bird is Norwich City's mascot?

251. What is the name of Everton's elephant mascot?
252. Which sea creature is Brighton & Hove Albion's mascot?
253. What animal represents Sunderland AFC?
254. What was the mascot for the 2006 FIFA World Cup in Germany?
255. Which animal is Reading FC's mascot?
256. What is the name of Southampton FC's saint mascot?
257. Which animal represents Preston North End?
258. What was the mascot for the 2002 FIFA World Cup in Korea/Japan?
259. Which bird is West Bromwich Albion's mascot?
260. What is the name of Aston Villa's lion mascot?
261. Which animal represents Blackburn Rovers?
262. What was the mascot for the 1998 FIFA World Cup in France?
263. Which mythical creature is Wales' national team mascot?
264. What is the name of Liverpool FC's liver bird mascot?
265. Which animal represents Middlesbrough FC?
266. What was the mascot for the 2012 European Championship in Poland/Ukraine?
267. What is the name of Newcastle United's magpie mascot?
268. Which animal is Fulham FC's mascot?
269. What was the mascot for the 2008 European Championship in Austria/Switzerland?
270. Which creature represents Huddersfield Town?

271. What is the name of Burnley FC's bee mascot?
272. Which animal is Brentford FC's mascot?
273. What was the mascot for the 2004 European Championship in Portugal?
274. What is the name of Sheffield Wednesday's owl mascot?
275. Which animal represents Bristol City?
276. What was the mascot for the 2000 European Championship in Belgium/Netherlands?
277. What is the name of Charlton Athletic's robin mascot?
278. Which animal is Ipswich Town's mascot?
279. What was the mascot for the 1996 European Championship in England?
280. What is the name of Millwall's lion mascot?
281. Which animal represents Nottingham Forest?
282. What was the mascot for the 1994 FIFA World Cup in the USA?
283. What is the name of Queens Park Rangers' tiger mascot?

Soccer World Records

284. Which player has scored the most international goals?
285. Who holds the record for the most World Cup appearances?
286. Which player has played in the most World Cup editions?
287. Which player has the most UEFA Champions League titles?
288. Who holds the record for the most goals scored in a single World Cup tournament?
289. What is the record for the fastest hat-trick in a professional match?
290. Which player has the most career goals in top-level professional soccer?
291. What is the record for the most goals scored in a single World Cup match?
292. Who holds the record for the most Premier League goals scored?
293. Which team has won the most UEFA Champions League/European Cup titles?
294. What is the record for the most capped international player?
295. Who holds the record for the most goals scored in a single UEFA Champions League season?
296. Which player has the most Ballon d'Or awards?

297. What is the record for the longest unbeaten run in top-level professional soccer?
298. Who holds the record for the most goals scored in a single La Liga season?
299. Which team has the most FIFA Club World Cup titles?
300. Which player has the most MLS career goals?
301. What is the record for the most goals scored in a single European Championship tournament?
302. Who holds the record for the most career assists in the Premier League?
303. Which team has the most consecutive league titles in a top-level professional league?
304. What is the record for the most penalty kicks scored in a single World Cup shootout?
305. Who holds the record for the most goals scored for a single club?
306. Which player has the most international appearances for their national team?
307. What is the record for the longest unbeaten run by a team in top-level professional soccer?
308. Who holds the record for the most goals scored in a single UEFA Champions League match?
309. Which team has the most FIFA World Cup titles?

310. What is the record for the oldest player to score in a World Cup match?
311. Who holds the record for the most goals scored in a single La Liga season?
312. Which player has the most career goals scored in UEFA national team competitions?
313. What is the record for the most goals scored in a single UEFA European Championship tournament?
314. Who holds the record for the most goals scored in a single Premier League season?
315. Which team has the most FIFA Club World Cup appearances?
316. What is the record for the youngest player to score in a World Cup match?
317. Who holds the record for the most career goals scored in the UEFA Champions League?
318. Which player has the most Golden Ball (best player) awards at the World Cup?
319. What is the record for the most goals scored in a single Copa Libertadores tournament?
320. Who holds the record for the most career MLS goals?
321. Which team has the most consecutive home wins in top-level professional soccer?
322. What is the record for the longest winning streak in top-level professional soccer?

323. Which player has the most career UEFA Super Cup appearances?

324. Which team has the most consecutive UEFA Champions League/European Cup titles?

325. What is the record for the most goals scored in a single MLS season?

326. Who holds the record for the most career appearances in the UEFA Champions League?

327. Which player has the most career goals scored in CONMEBOL tournaments?

328. What is the record for the most goals scored in a single international match?

Soccer Stadiums

329. Which stadium has the largest capacity in the world for a soccer match?
330. What is the name of the stadium that hosts the UEFA Champions League final?
331. Which stadium hosted the 2022 FIFA World Cup final in Qatar?
332. What is the name of the stadium that serves as the home ground for Barcelona FC?
333. Which stadium was the venue for the 1966 FIFA World Cup final in England?
334. What is the name of the stadium that hosts the annual MLS Cup final?
335. Which stadium in Italy is known for its iconic circular design?
336. What is the name of the stadium that serves as the home ground for Real Madrid FC?
337. Which stadium hosted the 2010 FIFA World Cup final in South Africa?
338. What is the name of the stadium that hosts the annual FA Cup final in England?
339. Which stadium in Germany has the highest average attendance in the Bundesliga?

340. What is the name of the stadium that hosted the 1998 FIFA World Cup final in France?
341. Which stadium in the Netherlands is known for its unique retractable roof?
342. What is the name of the stadium that serves as the home ground for Manchester United FC?
343. Which stadium in Brazil hosted the 2014 FIFA World Cup opening match?
344. What is the name of the stadium that hosts the annual Supercup final in Germany?
345. Which stadium in Spain is known for its steep stands and intimidating atmosphere?
346. What is the name of the stadium that hosted the 1986 FIFA World Cup final in Mexico?
347. Which stadium in Italy is nicknamed "the San Siro"?
348. What is the name of the stadium that hosts the annual Coppa Italia final in Italy?
349. Which stadium in England has the largest capacity outside of London?
350. What is the name of the stadium that hosted the 2006 FIFA World Cup final in Germany?
351. Which stadium in France is known for its iconic design with a retractable roof?

352. What is the name of the stadium that serves as the home ground for Juventus FC?
353. Which stadium in England is nicknamed "the Theatre of Dreams"?
354. What is the name of the stadium that hosted the 2018 FIFA World Cup final in Russia?
355. Which stadium in Argentina is known as the "Bombonera"?
356. What is the name of the stadium that serves as the home ground for Bayern Munich FC?
357. Which stadium in Portugal hosted the 2004 UEFA European Championship final?
358. What is the name of the stadium that hosts the annual DFB-Pokal final in Germany?

Soccer Technology

359. What technology was introduced to determine whether a ball has crossed the goal line?
360. Which video technology system was implemented to assist referees in making decisions?
361. What type of chips are embedded in modern soccer balls for data collection?
362. Which technology is used to track player movements and collect performance data during matches?
363. What system is used to communicate between referees during a match?
364. Which technology is used to create virtual offside lines for TV broadcasts?
365. What type of grass technology is often used in modern soccer stadiums?
366. Which technology is used to analyze ball spin and trajectory?
367. What type of cameras are used for high-speed replay analysis in soccer?
368. Which technology is used for fan engagement through stadium Wi-Fi and mobile apps?
369. What type of sensors are used in shin guards to collect player data?

370. Which technology is used for virtual reality training in soccer?
371. What type of software is commonly used for match analysis and tactics?
372. Which technology is used for automated highlights generation in soccer broadcasts?
373. What type of drones are used for aerial filming of soccer matches and training sessions?
374. Which technology is used for measuring the physical condition of players?
375. What type of technology is used for creating personalized training programs for players?
376. Which technology is used for predicting injuries in soccer players?
377. What type of artificial intelligence is used in soccer scouting and player recruitment?
378. Which technology is used for simulating crowd noise in empty stadiums?
379. What type of technology is used for ticket sales and access control in soccer stadiums?
380. Which technology is used for monitoring pitch conditions and maintenance?
381. What type of technology is used for fan voting systems during matches?

382. Which technology is used for creating 3D models of players for video games?
383. What type of technology is used for measuring ball pressure and temperature?
384. Which technology is used for tracking referee movements during matches?
385. What type of technology is used for creating virtual advertising boards in broadcasts?
386. Which technology is used for monitoring hydration levels in players?
387. What type of technology is used for improving the visibility of pitch markings?
388. Which technology is used for creating immersive fan experiences in stadiums?

Soccer Positions

389. What position typically wears the number 1 jersey?
390. Which position is responsible for preventing goals?
391. What is the primary role of a striker?
392. Which position is often referred to as a "playmaker"?
393. What is the main responsibility of a center-back?
394. Which position is commonly known as a "winger"?
395. What does a defensive midfielder typically do?
396. Which position is often called the "sweeper"?
397. What is the role of a full-back in modern soccer?
398. Which position is sometimes referred to as a "false nine"?
399. What is the primary duty of a goalkeeper coach?
400. Which job is responsible for overall team strategy and tactics?
401. What does a soccer scout typically do?
402. Which position in management oversees player transfers?
403. What is the role of a physio in a soccer team?
404. Which job involves analyzing opponent tactics and strategies?
405. What does a soccer agent do?
406. Which position on the coaching staff focuses on fitness?
407. What is the role of a soccer referee?
408. Which job involves maintaining the pitch and stadium?
409. What does a soccer nutritionist do?

410. Which position is responsible for team selection and tactics during a match?
411. What is the role of a soccer club's CEO?
412. Which job involves overseeing youth development in a club?
413. What does a video analyst do in soccer?
414. Which position is often called the "number 10"?
415. What is the primary role of a box-to-box midfielder?
416. Which coaching position focuses specifically on goalkeepers?
417. What does a soccer club's marketing director do?
418. Which job involves managing a club's finances?
419. What is the role of a soccer psychologist?
420. Which position is sometimes referred to as a "target man"?
421. What does a soccer data analyst typically do?
422. Which job involves liaising between players and management?
423. What is the role of a soccer club's community outreach manager?
424. Which position is often called the "anchor" in midfield?
425. What does a kit manager do in a soccer team?
426. Which job involves overseeing a club's medical department?
427. What is the role of a soccer club's social media manager?
428. Which position is sometimes referred to as a "trequartista"?

Messi and Ronaldo

429. In which country was Lionel Messi born?
430. What is the name of the club where Cristiano Ronaldo began his professional career?
431. How old was Messi when he joined FC Barcelona's youth academy, La Masia?
432. Which club did Ronaldo play for before joining Manchester United in 2003?
433. What medical condition did Messi overcome as a child, and how did it impact his early career?
434. How many Ballon d'Or awards has Cristiano Ronaldo won?
435. What is the significance of Messi's debut goal for FC Barcelona?
436. Which club did Ronaldo transfer to after leaving Manchester United in 2009?
437. What record did Messi break in the 2011-2012 La Liga season?
438. How many goals did Ronaldo score during his time at Real Madrid?
439. What is Messi's jersey number at FC Barcelona, and why is it significant?
440. What was Ronaldo's role in helping Portugal win the 2016 UEFA European Championship?

441. How did Messi's performance in the 2014 FIFA World Cup impact his international career?
442. What is the name of the club Ronaldo joined after leaving Real Madrid in 2018?
443. How many goals did Messi score in his final season at FC Barcelona?
444. What philanthropic work is Ronaldo known for outside of football?
445. What was the transfer fee paid by Paris Saint-Germain to acquire Messi in 2021?
446. How many goals did Ronaldo score on his return to Manchester United in 2021?
447. Who is Antonela Roccuzzo?
448. How many Champions League titles has Ronaldo won, and with which clubs?
449. Which city is Messi's hometown city?
450. How did Ronaldo's move to Juventus impact the Serie A and Italian football?
451. How many goals did Messi score in Argentina's victory in the 2021 Copa América?
452. Ronaldo's influence extended beyond football into fashion and business ventures. What fields has Ronaldo ventured into?

Soccer Moves

453. What is the basic technique used to move the ball around the field with your feet?

454. Name a popular dribbling move used to change direction quickly.

455. What is the term for using your body to protect the ball from defenders?

456. What is a common dribbling technique used to deceive defenders by playing the ball through their legs?

457. What type of pass is typically used to distribute the ball over long distances?

458. What is the name of a pass played through the final defensive line?

459. What is the importance of backspin in passing?

460. What is a common passing technique used to play the ball back towards your team's defense?

461. What is the area of the goal where a shot is most likely to go into the net if placed there?

462. What technique is often used to place a shot with power and precision?

463. Name a type of shot that is often used from outside the penalty area.

464. What is the term for a tackle where you slide on the ground to dispossess an opponent?

465. Why is it important to tackle cleanly and avoid fouling?

466. What is the term for a tackle that stops play?

467. What is the importance of timing in tackling?

468. What is the name of the area in front of the goal where the goalkeeper can handle the ball?

469. Name a common goalkeeping technique used to stop a shot.

470. What is the name of the skill where you use your head to control the ball?

471. What type of shot does a soccer player use when he shoots a ball that is in the air?

472. What type of shot does a soccer player use when he shoots a ball that just bounced off the ground?

Soccer Gear

473. What is the most essential piece of equipment in soccer?
474. What type of footwear is specifically designed for soccer players?
475. Name the protective gear worn by goalkeepers.
476. What is the purpose of shin guards?
477. What is the typical material used for soccer balls?
478. What is the name of the shirt worn by soccer players?
479. What is the name of the rectangular area where soccer matches are played?
480. What is the name of the area in front of the goal where the goalkeeper can handle the ball?
481. What is the name of the circular area around the penalty spot?
482. What is the name of the small bag used by players to carry their equipment?
483. What are the two cards that the referee carries with them?
484. What is the name of the device used by referees to communicate with the linesmen?

Soccer Fitness/Injury

485. What is the most common soccer injury?
486. What soccer injury mostly affects the knee?
487. What is the primary energy system used in soccer matches?
488. What type of training is best for improving cardiovascular fitness in soccer?
489. Name a popular cardiovascular training method for soccer players.
490. What is the recommended heart rate zone for soccer players during training?
491. Name a common strength training exercise for soccer players.
492. How does plyometric training improve strength and power?
493. Name a popular stretching technique for soccer players.
494. What is the difference between static and dynamic stretching?
495. Name a common drill to improve speed in soccer.
496. What are the most essential nutrients for soccer players?
497. What is the importance of hydration in soccer?
498. How can proper nutrition improve energy levels and performance?
499. What should soccer players avoid eating before a match?
500. How often should soccer players eat throughout the day?

Answers

1. 90 minutes, divided into two 45-minute halves.
2. 11 players.
3. When the ball fully crosses the goal line.
4. When the ball fully crosses the sideline.
5. Only the goalkeepers.
6. For fouls committed inside the penalty area.
7. 12 yards (11 meters).
8. When the defending team puts the ball out over their own goal line.
9. It must touch another player before entering the goal.
10. Yellow cards are warnings, red cards result in immediate dismissal.
11. It equals a red card, resulting in dismissal.
12. When the attacking team puts the ball out over the defending team's goal line.
13. 9.15 meters (10 yards).
14. When a player deliberately handles the ball with their hand/arm, or the ball hits the arm in an unnatural position.
15. Between 100-130 yards long and 50-100 yards wide.
16. No, players cannot be offside in their own half.
17. Typically, 18 players, including substitutes.

18. 7 players.
19. Two 15-minute periods.
20. The match goes to a penalty shootout.
21. 6 seconds.
22. The referee allows play to continue when the fouled team retains possession.
23. At least 9.15 meters (10 yards).
24. A method of restarting play after a stoppage where the referee is uncertain who should start. The referee drops the ball between two players, and two players from opposing sides try to kick the ball.
25. Yes.
26. One main referee and two assistant referees (linesmen).
27. To assist the main referee, manage substitutions and determine stoppage time.
28. No.
29. 12 centimeters (5 inches).
30. Through "stoppage time" added by the referee.
31. A deliberate foul to prevent a clear goal-scoring opportunity or gain some other form of advantage, which can result in a red card.
32. No, it results in a corner kick for the opposing team.
33. The kicker cannot touch the ball again until it has touched another player.

34. Yes, if the back-pass was intentional by a player on his team and was made with the foot.
35. When a team takes a free kick without waiting for the referee's whistle.
36. No.
37. A line of defending players positioned to block a free kick.
38. One.
39. No, once play restarts, the decision cannot be changed.
40. Yes.
41. 5 substitutions.
42. Yes, from the moment the referee enters the field of play.
43. Video Assistant Referee.
44. VAR can be used to check for offsides, penalties, direct red cards (not two yellow cards) and for mistaken identity (referee sending off wrong player).
45. Pelé.
46. Miroslav Klose.
47. Johan Cruyff.
48. Lionel Messi.
49. Lev Yashin.
50. Roberto Baggio.
51. Harry Kane.
52. Zico.
53. Diego Maradona.

54. Pelé.
55. José Mourinho
56. Gerd Müller.
57. Fabio Cannavaro.
58. Cristiano Ronaldo.
59. Michel Platini.
60. Ferenc Puskás.
61. Ronaldo (Brazilian).
62. Pelé.
63. Johan Cruyff.
64. Mohamed Salah.
65. Paul Gascoigne.
66. Roger Milla.
67. Uruguay.
68. Franz Beckenbauer.
69. Eusébio.
70. Pelé.
71. Gianluigi Buffon.
72. Lionel Messi.
73. Zinedine Zidane.
74. Pele.
75. Cristiano Ronaldo.
76. Lionel Messi.
77. Erling Haaland.

78. Kylian Mbappé.

79. Mohamed Salah.

80. Kevin De Bruyne.

81. Robert Lewandowski.

82. Vinícius Júnior.

83. Harry Kane.

84. Manuel Neuer.

85. Paul Pogba.

86. Virgil van Dijk.

87. Eden Hazard.

88. Gianluigi Donnarumma.

89. Bruno Fernandes.

90. Rodri.

91. Sadio Mané.

92. Ferland Mendy.

93. Ángel Di María.

94. Trent Alexander-Arnold.

95. Alisson Becker.

96. Luka Modrić.

97. Raphaël Varane.

98. João Cancelo.

99. Thomas Müller.

100. Pedri.

101. Jude Bellingham.

102. Cody Gakpo.
103. Marco Verratti.
104. Thibaut Courtois.
105. Manchester United.
106. Real Madrid.
107. Juventus.
108. Bayern Munich.
109. Ajax Amsterdam.
110. Benfica.
111. Liverpool.
112. Real Madrid.
113. AC Milan.
114. Paris Saint-Germain (PSG).
115. Rangers.
116. Santos.
117. River Plate.
118. Chelsea.
119. Barcelona.
120. Borussia Dortmund.
121. Inter Milan.
122. Fenerbahçe.
123. Manchester City.
124. Athletic Bilbao.
125. Ajax Amsterdam.

126. FC Porto.
127. AS Roma.
128. TSV 1860 Munich.
129. Arsenal.
130. Real Betis.
131. Olympique Lyonnais.
132. Rangers.
133. Corinthians.
134. Boca Juniors.
135. Manchester United.
136. Barcelona.
137. Torino.
138. Borussia Dortmund.
139. Feyenoord.
140. Sporting CP.
141. Tottenham Hotspur.
142. Atlético Madrid.
143. Fiorentina.
144. Olympique de Marseille.
145. Celtic.
146. Flamengo.
147. Racing Club.
148. Aston Villa.
149. Valencia CF.

150. Manchester United.
151. Brazil (5 titles).
152. 1930.
153. Miroslav Klose (Germany, 16 goals).
154. Qatar.
155. Luka Modrić (Croatia).
156. Cameroon (1990).
157. 1991.
158. Netherlands (3 finals, no wins).
159. Marta (Brazil, 17 goals).
160. Uruguay.
161. FIFA World Cup Trophy.
162. Lothar Matthäus (Germany, 5 tournaments).
163. Al Rihla.
164. Japan and South Korea (co-hosted).
165. Diego Maradona (Argentina).
166. Brazil.
167. 1998.
168. James Rodríguez (Colombia).
169. China.
170. Austria 7-5 Switzerland (1954).
171. Pelé (Brazil, 3 World Cups).
172. South Africa.
173. Pelé (Brazil, 17 years old in 1958).

174. 1982.

175. France.

176. Mario Götze.

177. Canada, United States, and Mexico (co-hosting).

178. It was the first World Cup to be hosted by two countries (Korea and Japan).

179. Emiliano Martínez (Argentina).

180. Jovan Kirovski.

181. 1994.

182. Claudio Reyna.

183. Major League Soccer (MLS).

184. Mia Hamm.

185. 1991.

186. Los Angeles.

187. Landon Donovan and Clint Dempsey.

188. MLS Cup.

189. Bruce Arena.

190. Seattle Sounders FC (in 2022).

191. Carlos Vela.

192. Brandi Chastain (in the penalty shootout).

193. Exploria Stadium (often referred to as their unofficial home in recent years).

194. Clint Dempsey.

195. Kasey Keller.

196. Kristine Lilly.

197. 1996.

198. The Stars and Stripes.

199. D.C. United.

200. Clint Dempsey.

201. John Harkes.

202. National Women's Soccer League (NWSL).

203. 109,318 (Michigan Stadium)

204. England.

205. Ramón Unzaga (Chile).

206. Notts County (England).

207. 1904.

208. Pelé.

209. 1866.

210. Soviet Union.

211. George Weah (Liberia).

212. Pele's Soccer (1980).

213. Manchester United (1998-99 season).

214. Sadik Kocadon (2 minutes 13 seconds, Turkey, 2019).

215. 1992.

216. Mexico (1970).

217. Giuseppe Savoldi (from Bologna to Napoli in 1975).

218. 1992.

219. Real Madrid (14 titles as of 2023).

220. Johan Cruyff.
221. 1970 (World Cup in Mexico).
222. Great Britain (1908).
223. Cristiano Ronaldo.
224. 1937 (Arsenal vs Arsenal Reserves).
225. Santos FC (Brazil).
226. Franz Beckenbauer (West Germany).
227. 1955 (as European Cup, rebranded to Champions League in 1992).
228. Uruguay
229. Peter Schmeichel (for Aston Villa against Everton in 2001).
230. Brazil (1994 against Italy).
231. 1984.
232. Cristiano Ronaldo.
233. Corinthians (Brazil) in 2000.
234. Lion (Three Lions).
235. Super Victor (an anthropomorphic boy with superpowers).
236. Gunnersaurus.
237. Filbert Fox.
238. Fred the Red.
239. Pete the Eagle.
240. Harry the Hornet.
241. Fuleco (an armadillo).
242. Stamford the Lion.

243. Chirpy the Cockerel.
244. Zabivaka (a wolf).
245. Cyril the Swan.
246. Rammie the Ram.
247. Hammerhead.
248. Wolfie.
249. Zakumi (a leopard).
250. Captain Canary.
251. Changy the Elephant.
252. Gully the Seagull.
253. Samson the Cat.
254. Goleo VI (a lion).
255. Kingsley Royal.
256. Super Saint and Sammy Saint.
257. Deepdale Duck.
258. Ato, Kaz, and Nik.
259. Baggie Bird.
260. Hercules the Lion.
261. Rovers Teddy Rover the Dog.
262. Footix (a rooster).
263. Draig (a dragon).
264. Mighty Red.
265. Roary the Lion.
266. Slavek and Slavko (twins).

267. Monty Magpie.
268. Billy the Badger.
269. Trix and Flix (twins).
270. Terry the Terrier.
271. Bertie Bee.
272. Buzz Bee.
273. Kinas (a boy).
274. Ozzie the Owl.
275. Robin.
276. Benelucky.
277. Floyd the Robin.
278. Bluey the Horse.
279. Goaliath (a lion).
280. Zampa the Lion.
281. Robin Hood.
282. Striker (a dog).
283. Jude the Cat.
284. Cristiano Ronaldo (140 goals as of 2024)
285. Lionel Messi (Argentina, 26 appearances).
286. Cristiano Ronaldo and Lionel Messi.
287. Gento (6 titles with Real Madrid).
288. Just Fontaine (France, 13 goals in 1958).
289. Alex Torr (70 seconds)
290. Cristiano Ronaldo (890 goals and going).

291. Hungary 10-1 El Salvador (1982 World Cup).
292. Alan Shearer (260 goals).
293. Real Madrid (15 titles as of 2024).
294. Cristiano Ronaldo
295. Cristiano Ronaldo (17 goals in 2013-14 season).
296. Lionel Messi (8 Ballon d'Or awards).
297. Celtic FC (62 games unbeaten, 1916-1917 to 1917-1918).
298. Lionel Messi (50 goals in 2011-12 La Liga season).
299. Real Madrid (7 titles).
300. Chris Wondolowski.
301. Michel Platini (9 goals in 1984).
302. Ryan Giggs
303. Skonto FC
304. West Germany (12 against France in 1982).
305. Lionel Messi (672 goals for Barcelona).
306. Cristiano Ronaldo
307. AC Milan (58 games unbeaten).
308. Lionel Messi (5 goals for Barcelona vs Bayer Leverkusen in 2012).
309. Brazil (5 titles).
310. Essam El-Hadary (Egypt, 45 years 161 days in 2018).
311. Lionel Messi (50 goals in 2011-12 La Liga season).
312. Cristiano Ronaldo (140 goals).
313. Michel Platini (9 goals in 1984).

314. Erling Haaland
315. Real Madrid (7 appearances).
316. Manuel Rosas (Mexico, 17 years 93 days in 1930).
317. Cristiano Ronaldo (140 goals).
318. Lionel Messi (7 awards).
319. Daniel Onega
320. Chris Wondolowski (172 goals).
321. Bayern Munich (73 consecutive home wins).
322. Real Madrid (wins from 2014-2017).
323. Alessandro Costacurta
324. Real Madrid (3 consecutive titles, 2016-2018).
325. Carlos Vela.
326. Cristiano Ronaldo
327. Pelé (CONMEBOL tournaments, 48 goals).
328. Australia 31-0 American Samoa (2001).
329. Rungrado 1st of May Stadium (North Korea, 114,000 capacity).
330. The stadium changes every year.
331. Lusail Iconic Stadium (Lusail, Qatar).
332. Camp Nou (Barcelona, Spain).
333. Wembley Stadium (London, England).
334. Banc of California Stadium (Los Angeles, USA).
335. Stadio Olympico (Rome, Italy).
336. Santiago Bernabéu Stadium (Madrid, Spain).
337. Soccer City (Johannesburg, South Africa).

338. Wembley Stadium (London, England).
339. Signal Iduna Park (Dortmund, Germany).
340. Stade de France (Paris, France).
341. Johan Cruyff Arena (Amsterdam, Netherlands).
342. Old Trafford (Manchester, England).
343. Arena Corinthians (São Paulo, Brazil).
344. Allianz Arena (Munich, Germany).
345. Camp Nou (Barcelona, Spain).
346. Estadio Azteca (Mexico City, Mexico).
347. Stadio Giuseppe Meazza (Milan, Italy).
348. Stadio Olimpico (Rome, Italy).
349. Old Trafford (Manchester, England).
350. Olympiastadion (Berlin, Germany).
351. Stade de France (Saint-Denis, France).
352. Allianz Stadium (Turin, Italy).
353. Old Trafford (Manchester, England).
354. Luzhniki Stadium (Moscow, Russia).
355. Estadio Alberto J. Armando (Buenos Aires, Argentina).
356. Allianz Arena (Munich, Germany).
357. Estádio da Luz (Lisbon, Portugal).
358. Olympiastadion (Berlin, Germany).
359. Goal-line technology (GLT).
360. Video Assistant Referee (VAR).
361. RFID chips.

362. GPS tracking systems and optical tracking cameras.
363. Wireless communication headsets.
364. Hawk-Eye technology.
365. Hybrid grass systems (combination of natural/artificial grass).
366. Ball flight tracking systems (e.g., Hawk-Eye).
367. Ultra-high-speed cameras (1000+ frames per second).
368. Stadium-wide Wi-Fi and custom mobile applications.
369. Accelerometers and gyroscopes.
370. VR headsets and software (e.g., STRIVR, Beyond Sports).
371. Opta Sports or Wyscout analytics software.
372. AI-powered video analysis and editing software.
373. Autonomous drones with stabilized cameras.
374. Bioimpedance analysis and heart rate variability monitors.
375. AI-driven performance analysis software.
376. Machine learning algorithms analyzing player data.
377. AI-powered player performance prediction models.
378. Artificial crowd noise systems.
379. RFID or NFC-based ticketing systems.
380. IoT sensors and weather stations.
381. Mobile voting apps and in-stadium polling systems.
382. 3D scanning and motion capture technology.
383. Smart ball technology with embedded sensors.
384. Wearable GPS trackers for officials.
385. Augmented reality (AR) advertising technology.

386. Sweat analysis patches or smart water bottles.

387. LED lighting systems for pitch markings.

388. Augmented reality (AR) apps for fan engagement.

389. Goalkeeper.s

390. Goalkeeper.

391. Score goals.

392. Attacking midfielder.

393. Defend against opposition attacks.

394. Wide midfielder or forward.

395. Protect the defense and break up opposition attacks.

396. A defensive position behind the center-backs.

397. Defend and contribute to attacking play.

398. A striker who drops deep into midfield.

399. Train and develop goalkeepers.

400. Head coach/manager.

401. Identify talented players for potential recruitment.

402. Director of Football or Sporting Director.

403. Treat and rehabilitate injured players; Injury prevention.

404. Opposition analyst.

405. Represent players in contract negotiations / transfers.

406. Fitness coach.

407. Enforce the rules of the game during matches.

408. Groundskeeper.

409. Plan and monitor players' diets and nutrition.

410. Manager/Head coach.
411. Oversee overall club operations and strategy.
412. Academy Director.
413. Analyze match footage for tactical insights.
414. Attacking midfielder.
415. Contribute to both attack and defense across the entire field
416. Goalkeeper coach.
417. Manage the club's brand and promotional activities.
418. Chief Financial Officer (CFO).
419. Provide mental support and strategies for players.
420. A tall, strong striker who holds up play.
421. Collect and interpret statistical data on players and teams.
422. Team captain or player liaison officer.
423. Organize and manage community engagement programs.
424. Defensive midfielder.
425. Manage team uniforms and equipment.
426. Head of Medical Department.
427. Manage the club's presence on social media platforms.
428. A creative attacking midfielder (Italian term).
429. Argentina
430. Sporting CP
431. 13 years old
432. Sporting Lisbon
433. Growth hormone deficiency

434. 5
435. First official goal for Barcelona at age 17
436. Real Madrid
437. 50 goals in a La Liga season
438. 450 goals
439. Number 10; symbolizes playmaking and leadership
440. Captained Portugal; pivotal in knockout stages
441. Led Argentina to the final; won the Golden Ball
442. Juventus
443. 30 goals
444. Extensive charity work, including donations to hospitals
445. Free transfer; Messi signed with PSG due to financial constraints at Barcelona
446. Ronaldo scored 24 goals in his first season back
447. Messi's Childhood sweetheart; they married in 2017
448. 5; Manchester United, Real Madrid
449. Rosario is his hometown; deeply connected to his roots
450. Increased viewership and competition in Serie A
451. Scored 4 goals
452. Successful fashion line, CR7 brand, hotels, and more
453. Dribbling
454. Cruyff turn
455. Shielding
456. Nutmeg

457. Long ball or Lob
458. Through ball or Sweeper pass
459. Backspin helps the ball stay low and avoid defenders.
460. Reverse pass
461. Top corners
462. Instep shot
463. Curler or Free-kick
464. Sliding tackle
465. Tackling cleanly prevents injuries and fouls.
466. Foul
467. Timing is crucial to dispossess the opponent without fouling.
468. Six-yard box or Penalty area
469. Heading
470. Volley
471. Half Volley
472. Soccer ball
473. Cleats
474. Goalkeeper gloves, jersey, shorts, and pants
475. Protect the shins from injury from other cleats
476. Leather/synthetic materials
477. Jersey
478. Soccer field
479. Six-yard box or Penalty area
480. Penalty arc

481. Kit bag
482. Yellow Card and Red Card
483. Walkie-talkie or Headset
484. Ankle sprain
485. ACL Tear
486. Anaerobic
487. Interval Training
488. Fartlek Training
489. 70-85% of maximum heart rate.
490. Squats, lunges, planks, and core exercises
491. Plyometric training involves explosive movements, improving power and explosiveness.
492. Dynamic stretching
493. Static stretching involves holding a stretch for a period of time, while dynamic stretching involves active movements.
494. Speed and Agility Ladder Drills
495. Carbohydrates, protein, fats, vitamins, minerals, and water
496. Hydration is essential for maintaining performance and preventing dehydration.
497. Proper nutrition provides energy, fuels recovery, and supports overall health.
498. Avoid heavy, greasy, or spicy foods before a match.
499. Eat small, frequent meals throughout the day to maintain energy levels.

APPENDIX

Participant/Team Name / Team	Round 1 Basic Soccer	Round 2 Legends	Round 3 Clubs	Round 4 World Cup	Round 5 US Soccer	Round 6 World Rec	Round 7 Stadiums	Round 8 Technology	Round 9 Messi/Ronaldo	Round 10 Positions	Total
1											
2											
3											
4											
5											
6											
7											
8											

Participant/Team Name / Team	Round 1 Basic Soccer	Round 2 Legends	Round 3 Clubs	Round 4 World Cup	Round 5 US Soccer	Round 6 World Rec	Round 7 Stadiums	Round 8 Technology	Round 9 Messi/Ronaldo	Round 10 Positions	Total
1											
2											
3											
4											
5											
6											
7											
8											

Participant/Team Name / Team	Round 1 Basic Soccer	Round 2 Legends	Round 3 Clubs	Round 4 World Cup	Round 5 US Soccer	Round 6 World Rec	Round 7 Stadiums	Round 8 Technology	Round 9 Messi/Ronaldo	Round 10 Positions	Total
1											
2											
3											
4											
5											
6											
7											
8											

Participant/Team Name / Team	Round 1 Basic Soccer	Round 2 Legends	Round 3 Clubs	Round 4 World Cup	Round 5 US Soccer	Round 6 World Rec	Round 7 Stadiums	Round 8 Technology	Round 9 Messi/Ronaldo	Round 10 Positions	Total
1											
2											
3											
4											
5											
6											
7											
8											

Participant/Team Name / Team	Round 1 Basic Soccer	Round 2 Legends	Round 3 Clubs	Round 4 World Cup	Round 5 US Soccer	Round 6 World Rec	Round 7 Stadiums	Round 8 Technology	Round 9 Messi/Ronaldo	Round 10 Positions	Total
1											
2											
3											
4											
5											
6											
7											
8											

Participant/Team Name / Team	Round 1 Basic Soccer	Round 2 Legends	Round 3 Clubs	Round 4 World Cup	Round 5 US Soccer	Round 6 World Rec	Round 7 Stadiums	Round 8 Technology	Round 9 Messi/Ronaldo	Round 10 Positions	Total
1											
2											
3											
4											
5											
6											
7											
8											

Participant/Team Name / Team	Round 1 Basic Soccer	Round 2 Legends	Round 3 Clubs	Round 4 World Cup	Round 5 US Soccer	Round 6 World Rec	Round 7 Stadiums	Round 8 Technology	Round 9 Messi/Ronaldo	Round 10 Positions	Total
1											
2											
3											
4											
5											
6											
7											
8											

Participant/Team Name / Team	Round 1 Basic Soccer	Round 2 Legends	Round 3 Clubs	Round 4 World Cup	Round 5 US Soccer	Round 6 World Rec	Round 7 Stadiums	Round 8 Technology	Round 9 Messi/Ronaldo	Round 10 Positions	Total
1											
2											
3											
4											
5											
6											
7											
8											

Participant/Team Name / Team	Round 1 Basic Soccer	Round 2 Legends	Round 3 Clubs	Round 4 World Cup	Round 5 US Soccer	Round 6 World Rec	Round 7 Stadiums	Round 8 Technology	Round 9 Messi/Ronaldo	Round 10 Positions	Total
1											
2											
3											
4											
5											
6											
7											
8											

Participant/Team Name / Team	Round 1 Basic Soccer	Round 2 Legends	Round 3 Clubs	Round 4 World Cup	Round 5 US Soccer	Round 6 World Rec	Round 7 Stadiums	Round 8 Technology	Round 9 Messi/Ronaldo	Round 10 Positions	Total
1											
2											
3											
4											
5											
6											
7											
8											

Participant/Team Name / Team	Round 1 Basic Soccer	Round 2 Legends	Round 3 Clubs	Round 4 World Cup	Round 5 US Soccer	Round 6 World Rec	Round 7 Stadiums	Round 8 Technology	Round 9 Messi/Ronaldo	Round 10 Positions	Total
1											
2											
3											
4											
5											
6											
7											
8											

Participant/Team Name / Team	Round 1 Basic Soccer	Round 2 Legends	Round 3 Clubs	Round 4 World Cup	Round 5 US Soccer	Round 6 World Rec	Round 7 Stadiums	Round 8 Technology	Round 9 Messi/Ronaldo	Round 10 Positions	Total
1											
2											
3											
4											
5											
6											
7											
8											

Participant/Team Name / Team	Round 1 Basic Soccer	Round 2 Legends	Round 3 Clubs	Round 4 World Cup	Round 5 US Soccer	Round 6 World Rec	Round 7 Stadiums	Round 8 Technology	Round 9 Messi/Ronaldo	Round 10 Positions	Total
1											
2											
3											
4											
5											
6											
7											
8											

Participant/Team Name / Team	Round 1 Basic Soccer	Round 2 Legends	Round 3 Clubs	Round 4 World Cup	Round 5 US Soccer	Round 6 World Rec	Round 7 Stadiums	Round 8 Technology	Round 9 Messi/Ronaldo	Round 10 Positions	Total
1											
2											
3											
4											
5											
6											
7											
8											

Participant/Team Name / Team	Round 1 Basic Soccer	Round 2 Legends	Round 3 Clubs	Round 4 World Cup	Round 5 US Soccer	Round 6 World Rec	Round 7 Stadiums	Round 8 Technology	Round 9 Messi/Ronaldo	Round 10 Positions	Total
1											
2											
3											
4											
5											
6											
7											
8											

Participant/Team Name / Team	Round 1 Basic Soccer	Round 2 Legends	Round 3 Clubs	Round 4 World Cup	Round 5 US Soccer	Round 6 World Rec	Round 7 Stadiums	Round 8 Technology	Round 9 Messi/Ronaldo	Round 10 Positions	Total
1											
2											
3											
4											
5											
6											
7											
8											

Participant/Team Name / Team	Round 1 Basic Soccer	Round 2 Legends	Round 3 Clubs	Round 4 World Cup	Round 5 US Soccer	Round 6 World Rec	Round 7 Stadiums	Round 8 Technology	Round 9 Messi/Ronaldo	Round 10 Positions	Total
1											
2											
3											
4											
5											
6											
7											
8											

Participant/Team Name / Team	Round 1 Basic Soccer	Round 2 Legends	Round 3 Clubs	Round 4 World Cup	Round 5 US Soccer	Round 6 World Rec	Round 7 Stadiums	Round 8 Technology	Round 9 Messi/Ronaldo	Round 10 Positions	Total
1											
2											
3											
4											
5											
6											
7											
8											

Participant/Team Name / Team	Round 1 Basic Soccer	Round 2 Legends	Round 3 Clubs	Round 4 World Cup	Round 5 US Soccer	Round 6 World Rec	Round 7 Stadiums	Round 8 Technology	Round 9 Messi/Ronaldo	Round 10 Positions	Total
1											
2											
3											
4											
5											
6											
7											
8											

Participant/Team Name / Team	Round 1 Basic Soccer	Round 2 Legends	Round 3 Clubs	Round 4 World Cup	Round 5 US Soccer	Round 6 World Rec	Round 7 Stadiums	Round 8 Technology	Round 9 Messi/Ronaldo	Round 10 Positions	Total
1											
2											
3											
4											
5											
6											
7											
8											

Participant/Team Name / Team	Round 1 Basic Soccer	Round 2 Legends	Round 3 Clubs	Round 4 World Cup	Round 5 US Soccer	Round 6 World Rec	Round 7 Stadiums	Round 8 Technology	Round 9 Messi/Ronaldo	Round 10 Positions	Total
1											
2											
3											
4											
5											
6											
7											
8											

Participant/Team Name / Team	Round 1 Basic Soccer	Round 2 Legends	Round 3 Clubs	Round 4 World Cup	Round 5 US Soccer	Round 6 World Rec	Round 7 Stadiums	Round 8 Technology	Round 9 Messi/Ronaldo	Round 10 Positions	Total
1											
2											
3											
4											
5											
6											
7											
8											

Participant/Team Name / Team	Round 1 Basic Soccer	Round 2 Legends	Round 3 Clubs	Round 4 World Cup	Round 5 US Soccer	Round 6 World Rec	Round 7 Stadiums	Round 8 Technology	Round 9 Messi/Ronaldo	Round 10 Positions	Total
1											
2											
3											
4											
5											
6											
7											
8											

Participant/Team Name / Team	Round 1 Basic Soccer	Round 2 Legends	Round 3 Clubs	Round 4 World Cup	Round 5 US Soccer	Round 6 World Rec	Round 7 Stadiums	Round 8 Technology	Round 9 Messi/Ronaldo	Round 10 Positions	Total
1											
2											
3											
4											
5											
6											
7											
8											

Participant/Team Name / Team	Round 1 Basic Soccer	Round 2 Legends	Round 3 Clubs	Round 4 World Cup	Round 5 US Soccer	Round 6 World Rec	Round 7 Stadiums	Round 8 Technology	Round 9 Messi/Ronaldo	Round 10 Positions	Total
1											
2											
3											
4											
5											
6											
7											
8											

Participant/Team Name / Team	Round 1 Basic Soccer	Round 2 Legends	Round 3 Clubs	Round 4 World Cup	Round 5 US Soccer	Round 6 World Rec	Round 7 Stadiums	Round 8 Technology	Round 9 Messi/Ronaldo	Round 10 Positions	Total
1											
2											
3											
4											
5											
6											
7											
8											

Participant/Team Name / Team	Round 1 Basic Soccer	Round 2 Legends	Round 3 Clubs	Round 4 World Cup	Round 5 US Soccer	Round 6 World Rec	Round 7 Stadiums	Round 8 Technology	Round 9 Messi/Ronaldo	Round 10 Positions	Total
1											
2											
3											
4											
5											
6											
7											
8											

Participant/Team Name / Team	Round 1 Basic Soccer	Round 2 Legends	Round 3 Clubs	Round 4 World Cup	Round 5 US Soccer	Round 6 World Rec	Round 7 Stadiums	Round 8 Technology	Round 9 Messi/Ronaldo	Round 10 Positions	Total
1											
2											
3											
4											
5											
6											
7											
8											

Participant/Team Name / Team	Round 1 Basic Soccer	Round 2 Legends	Round 3 Clubs	Round 4 World Cup	Round 5 US Soccer	Round 6 World Rec	Round 7 Stadiums	Round 8 Technology	Round 9 Messi/Ronaldo	Round 10 Positions	Total
1											
2											
3											
4											
5											
6											
7											
8											

Participant/Team Name / Team	Round 1 Basic Soccer	Round 2 Legends	Round 3 Clubs	Round 4 World Cup	Round 5 US Soccer	Round 6 World Rec	Round 7 Stadiums	Round 8 Technology	Round 9 Messi/Ronaldo	Round 10 Positions	Total
1											
2											
3											
4											
5											
6											
7											
8											

www.ingramcontent.com/pod-product-compliance
Lightning Source LLC
Chambersburg PA
CBHW071912070526
44583CB00016B/1956